W9-BWT-300

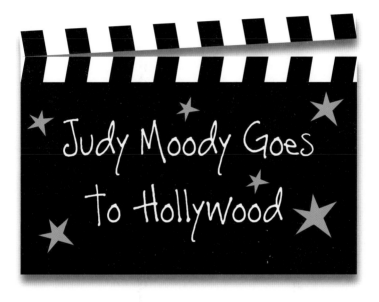

Judy Moody Goes to Hollywood

Above: Megan McDonald and Jordana Beatty
Opposite page: Garrett Ryan, Jordana Beatty, Taylar Hender, Preston Bailey

Judy Moody Goes to Hollywood

Behind the Scenes with Judy Moody and Friends

by Megan McDonald
with Richard Haynes
set photography by Suzanne Tenner

CANDLEWICK PRESS

Compilation and images copyright © 2011 by CBM Productions, LLC
Text copyright © 2011 by Megan McDonald

Based on the theatrical motion picture
Judy Moody and the NOT Bummer Summer,
produced by Smokewood Entertainment

Judy Moody®. Judy Moody is a registered trademark of Candlewick Press, Inc.
Judy Moody font copyright © 2003 by Peter H. Reynolds
Line drawings on pages 6, 8–9, and 10–13 copyright © 2000,
2001, 2005, and 2006 by Peter H. Reynolds
Other line drawings on pages 11 and 13 copyright © 2011 by Candlewick Press, Inc.

All rights reserved. No part of this book may be reproduced,
transmitted, or stored in an information retrieval system
in any form or by any means, graphic, electronic, or mechanical,
including photocopying, taping, and recording,
without prior written permission from the publisher.

First edition 2011

ISBN 978-0-7636-5551-8

11 12 13 14 15 16 LBM 10 9 8 7 6 5 4 3 2 1

Printed in Melrose Park, IL, U.S.A.

This book was typeset in Stone Informal and Judy Moody.

Candlewick Press
99 Dover Street
Somerville, Massachusetts 02144

visit us at www.candlewick.com

For Sarah

Judy Moody Gets Famous— for Real!

"IN A HOLLYWOOD MOOD"
by Judy Moody

Hey, everybody! I, Judy Moody, have some way-rare, mega-exciting news. Thrill-o-rama! You know how I've been trying to get famous for a while now? First it was a picture of my elbow in the newspaper. Then they spelled my name *Judy Muddy.* I thought I'd never ever EVER get famous.

But, guess what! There's now a movie all about—you guessed it—me, me, me, me, ME! For sure and absolute positive. It's called *Judy Moody and the NOT Bummer Summer.*

I, and nobody else but me, got the top-secret, WAY-behind-the-scenes inside poop-scoop about the making of the whole, entire movie. It's so uber-awesome I just had to give you a peek! From bike chases to Bigfoot races, tightropes to high hopes for the best summer ever—it's all here! Start turning the pages and earn thrill points as you go. One word says it all:

Super-cali-fragi-listic-expi-thrilla-delic!

THE MANY MOODS OF JUDY MOODY

Excited about a summer of thrills ahead. Down in the dumps when she has to say so long to her best friend. From mad moods to glad moods to sad moods, Judy Moody has felt them all. In fact, Judy has so many moods, it's like taking a ride on the Scream Monster roller coaster at Scare Devil Island Amusement Park!

* Happy
* Glad

* Unhappy
* Sad

* Grouchy
* Impossible

* Jealous
* Envy

* Curious
* Eager

* Frustrated
* Mad

* Joyful
* On Top of the World

WHO'S WHO

Finding the right actors and actresses to bring the characters created by Megan McDonald and drawn by Peter H. Reynolds to walking, talking life was the job of casting director Julie Ashton. She searched far and wide, high and low, day and night, and around the world for perfect matches!

Meet the Cast!

Illustrated Judy + Jordana Beatty = Movie Judy

Illustrated Stink + Parris Mosteller = Movie Stink

Illustrated Aunt Opal + Heather Graham = Movie Aunt Opal

Illustrated Mom + Janet Varney = Movie Mom

Illustrated Dad + Kristoffer Winters = Movie Dad

Illustrated Mr. Todd + Jaleel White = Movie Mr. Todd

Illustrated Frank Pearl + Preston Bailey = Movie Frank Pearl

Illustrated Amy Namey + Taylar Hender = Movie Amy Namey

Illustrated Rocky Zang + Garrett Ryan = Movie Rocky Zang

Illustrated Jessica Finch + Ashley Boettcher = Movie Jessica Finch

Illustrated Zeke + Jackson Odell = Movie Zeke

Illustrated Mr. Birnbaum + Robert Costanza = Movie Mr. Birnbaum

Illustrated Mrs. Birnbaum + Sharon Sachs = Movie Mrs. Birnbaum

Illustrated Mouse + Tails and Tux = Movie Mouse

A STAR IS BORN

The first Judy Moody book was published in April 2000. Since then, she has starred in at least twelve novels, two activity books, a journal, and now a movie! The book series has been published in more than twenty countries and languages. Ooh-la-la!

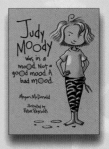

2000: first-ever cover

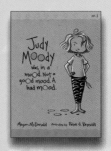

2005: a new look!

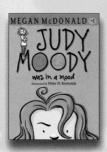

2010: the 10th anniversary edition!

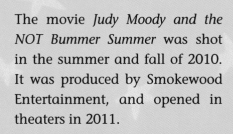

Judy Moody was in a mood. Not a good mood. A bad mood.

The movie *Judy Moody and the NOT Bummer Summer* was shot in the summer and fall of 2010. It was produced by Smokewood Entertainment, and opened in theaters in 2011.

Once Upon a Time . . .

It's been called the Toilet Paper Club. It's been called the Totally Presents Club. But just what exactly *is* the T.P. Club? And how did it all start?

Once upon a time, the author of the Judy Moody books, Megan McDonald, was a kid. She had four older sisters. The sisters always had secret clubs. One time, while they were on a family vacation, the sisters caught a toad. They convinced Megan to pick it up. She held it in her hand. In no time, she felt something warm and wet. Toad pee!

So Megan McDonald became a lifetime member of the Toad Pee Club. Just like Judy Moody, Stink, and her friends Rocky and Frank. Who will become the newest member of the Toad Pee Club? Mr. Todd? Jessica Finch? You'll have to watch the movie to find out!

You, too, can become a member of the Toad Pee Club. All you have to do is pick up a toad! And wait . . . Do you feel anything? Eeeuw!

T.P. Club meeting. Be there or be a square-pants.

Nice Toady!

JUDY "SCOOPS" MOODY TALKS TO

JM: So, you're the producer, huh? How did you even find out about me, then get the idea to turn me, Judy Moody, into a real-live big-screen MOVIE?

SSM: *When she was in second grade, my daughter, Camryn, brought home a book about you.*

JM: Cool beans! Say more.

SSM: *We read it together and laughed our pants off. I knew then that I wanted to turn your story into a feature film.*

JM: Are you, or anybody in your family, in the movie?

SSM: *My husband, Gary, is the cabdriver when Aunt Opal arrives. My daughter, Camryn, is the zombie cheerleader who calls you "Hairhead" in the movie-theater scene. And my son, Cable, is Lobster Boy in the movie theater. You also see him pop out of the bouncy castle.*

JM: Do you have ideas about more movies you want to make?

SSM: *Oh, I have tons. I want to make a romantic comedy, an action movie, a fully animated kids' film. But first, we're going to rock the sequel to Judy Moody. High five!*

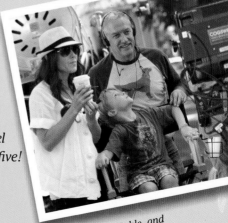

Sarah, Cable, and
Gary Magness

SARAH SIEGEL-MAGNESS, V.I.P. (aka VERY IMPORTANT PRODUCER)

Sarah Siegel-Magness, along with her husband, Gary Magness, is the producer of *Judy Moody and the NOT Bummer Summer,* which means that the idea to turn the Judy Moody series into a movie was hers! And it means that she made it all possible. First she hired Megan McDonald and Kathy Waugh to write the screenplay. Then she hired John Schultz to direct the movie. Then she hired the bazillion other people needed to make a movie. Sarah and her husband are the founders of the production company Smokewood Entertainment.

The whole family gets in a Judy Moody mood!

Cable, Lobster Boy!

Camryn, zombie cheerleader

Sarah and Camryn at the circus.

THE MEGA-RARE NOT BUMMER SUMMER DARE IS ON!

ROAR! It's not bad enough that Mom and Dad are heading to California, leaving Judy and Stink with Aunt Awful (er, Opal), but now Judy's two best friends are going Splitsville, too. Just when it looks like her summer is going to be BORing—eureka!—Judy comes up with the most thrill-a-delic plan ever. Get ready for a race involving tightrope walking, Scream Monster riding, and way more! Add in a treasure hunt for Judy's teacher, a midnight stakeout, a runaway ice-cream truck, and a dash of Bigfoot, and what have you got? Presto whammo, the Judy Moodiest summer ever!

Score your own Thrill Points!

Want to score some thrill points of your own? Look for the Thrill Points boxes or arrows as you read the book. The chart on page 144 will help you keep track!

Dare Chart designed by Brittany Macwhorter

Searching for Mr. Todd

You'll put me back together, right?

The Great Judy-a-Rini will not fallllll . . . !

WHAT WAS THAT?

Watch out for dead jellyfish!

Mine!

Scream Monsterrrrr!

Did somebody say
Poop Picnic?

A Midsummer Night's Scream

After him! Go-go-
go-go-go-go!

★ ★ ★ 21 ★ ★

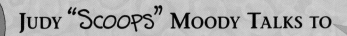

JUDY "SCOOPS" MOODY TALKS TO

JM: So, you're gonna play me on the big screen, huh?

JB: Yep. It's very exciting! RARE!

JM: Did you have to get your hair cut to look like me?

JB: Yes. That was REALLY scary. Also sad because I've never had a haircut, really, just a trim, and I've been trying to grow it really long forever.

JM: You're from Australia! Was it hard to learn to speak with an American accent?

JB: What really helped was coming to the United States and being around American kids. I had a dialect coach, too, Francie Brown, and she really helped me at the beginning with tons of difficult words and sayings.

JM: What's your favorite thing about the United States that you don't have in Australia?

JB: I got to chew mint-chip ice-cream gum! Also, I got to go to the American Girl store, which we don't have in Australia, and I started collecting Silly Bandz. I learned about geocaching and found my first treasure box in Hollywood! And I'm hoping to taste a s'more before I leave. We don't have those in Sydney.

JM: What do you like about playing . . . ME?

JB: You have an exciting life. You're always up for some sort of adventure. You're very keen to get things done—I like that. You have so many crazy ideas and such a good imagination.

JORDANA BEATTY (aka JUDY MOODY)

JM: I hate to brush my hair. How many times a day did you have to get your hair messed up to make it look like mine?

JB: *Between every single take. That probably adds up to about a hundred times a day!*

JM: What would you like to do that would be thrill-a-delic?

JB: *Swim with dolphins! Also, I'd love to go to Washington, D.C. And I'd like to see the Statue of Liberty someday.*

JM: In real life, do you think you're like me?

JB: *I like mood rings a lot, and I love to read Nancy Drew books, and purple is my favorite color. Also, I can raise one eyebrow like you do!*

JM/JB: Same-same!

The Bride of Frankenstein goes to school with Bill Clark, studio teacher.

With her parents,
Sean and Nerida

With her movie brother,
Parris Mosteller
(aka Stink)

Jordana shows off her book autographed by Megan McDonald AND Peter H. Reynolds! DOUBLE RARE!

Jordana Beatty, the young actress who plays Judy Moody, is an Aussie! That means she's from Australia. In order to play Judy Moody, Jordana had to learn how to speak with an American accent. The words she had the most trouble with?

- **jawbreaker** (In Australia, it's pronounced JOO-wah BRAY-kah.)
- **California**
- **idea**
- **Popsicle** (Jordana kept saying "popstickle.")
- **record**
- **Super-cali-fragi-listic-expi-thrilla-delic!**

Just as an athlete needs to warm up the body for a game or a meet, an actor or actress needs to warm up his or her mouth for a performance. Acting coaches on the set had the kids run through a bunch of tongue twisters. Here are a few they had to practice:

- Unique New York. You know you need unique New York.
- Any noise annoys an oyster, but a noisy noise annoys the oyster most.
- A box of biscuits, a box of mixed biscuits, and a biscuit mixer.

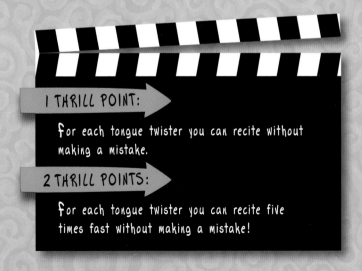

1 THRILL POINT:

For each tongue twister you can recite without making a mistake.

2 THRILL POINTS:

For each tongue twister you can recite five times fast without making a mistake!

Moody Squared

Mrs. Moody is played by Janet Varney. Mr. Moody is played by Kristoffer Winters. Here's a little quiz about the actors. Can you guess—Mom or Dad?

THRILL POINT For each correct answer!

1. Which actor is a comedian?
2. Which actor has played a high-school principal?
3. Which actor grew up in New Jersey?
4. Which actor starred on a fictional TV show called *One Car, Two Car, Red Car, Blue Car*?
5. Which actor starred in *Catwoman* with Halle Berry?
6. Which actor has blond hair in real life?
7. Which actor played a character named Zilbor?
8. Which actor has three aliases spelled three different ways?

Answers on page 136

DO NOT DISTURB

Welcome to the one-and-only room of Judy Moody! Have you ever wanted to live in a mini-museum? Judy is a collector of stuff, from Band-Aids to grouchy pencils, erasers to pizza tables. Take a tour of her bedroom on the next two pages and see what collections you can spot.

DO NOT DISTURB!

Rest of the → Judy Moody is spending the summer in her Room!

HEY KIDS!

CRAZY STRIPS ADHESIVE BANDAGES

25 STERILE STRIPS
5 SIZES

FREE TATTOO INSIDE!

BUG STRIP!

These props designed by Lauren Day and Brittany Macwhorter

2 THRILL POINTS:

For each of the items you find on the next two pages:

- Class 3T photo
- Snow globe collection
- Hedda Get Betta
- Me Collage
- Giraffe Award

Hey, John and Jordana! Where's the ceiling?

Judy "Scoops" Moody Talks to

A film director keeps the "big picture" in mind while also paying attention to every detail, from costumes to makeup to props to lighting to special effects and more. He works with the writer to polish a screenplay. He directs the actors in how to play their parts and say their lines. He instructs the crew about how a scene should be set up, lit, filmed, and edited. And the list goes on. Phew!

JM: How old were you when you made your first movie?

JS: *I was twelve years old when I made* Skateboard Story, *a short film.*

JM: So you've been making movies since you were twelve. When did you know that you wanted to be a movie director?

JS: *Well, I've always been a director, starting with* Skateboard Story. *The trick was turning what I loved doing into a paying job and keeping it fun. And I totally got to do that on* Judy Moody and the NOT Bummer Summer!

JM: What other films have you directed?

JS: *There's* Aliens in the Attic, When Zachary Beaver Came to Town, *and* Like Mike, *to name a few that kids might like.*

JM: What made you want to direct a film about me?

JS: *You have a great energy and spirit that kids of any age can relate to.*

JM: What was the most fun you had while making the movie?

John Schultz, Director

JS: *Surfing! Spending a day on a sunny beach teaching Preston Bailey to bodysurf and fighting those crazy waves! Also, seeing Jordana face the waves as they grew huge during her close-ups was unbelievable. She is so brave!*

JM: If a kid wants to be a movie director, what advice might you have for him or her?

JS: *Be a director now. Start making movies today. Draw each shot you will shoot, then get your hands on a camera. If you don't have a camera, put on a play with your friends.*

JM: What scene in the movie would you tell kids they absolutely, positively, for-sure can NOT miss?

JS: *I would tell them that they absolutely, positively, for-sure can NOT chicken out and close their eyes when Judy and Stink go into the woods at night to find Bigfoot!*

John checks out the camera and lighting setup for an indoor scene.

Reviewing film footage with Sarah Siegel-Magness, Megan McDonald, Richard Haynes, and Andrew Sugerman.

ZOMBIE MOVIE

"Beware of the Blob! It creeps, and leaps, and glides and slides . . ." Thrills! Chills! Blobs! Globs! In the 1950s, monster and alien movies became super popular. *Creature from the Black Lagoon* and *I Was a Teenage Frankenstein* were two blockbusters filmed in black and white when special effects were just beginning. John Schultz, the director, thought it would be fun to show a movie within a movie. So he decided to make his own black-and-white fifties-style zombie movie for Judy and Frank to watch at the Evil Creature Double Feature. All he needed was one screaming woman, a few undead zombies, and maybe, just maybe . . . a runaway eyeball!

2 THRILL POINTS:

If you watch one of John Schultz's earlier movies

4 THRILL POINTS:

If you watch two of John Schultz's earlier movies

6 THRILL POINTS:

If you watch three!

Storyboards

Do you like drawing comics? Then you could be a story-board artist! The director has to plan every shot and angle in the film. A storyboard artist takes the directors' rough sketches and draws the entire movie shot by shot. A random sampling of single storyboard frames:

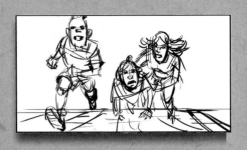

Full storyboard pages outlining part of a scene at the circus.

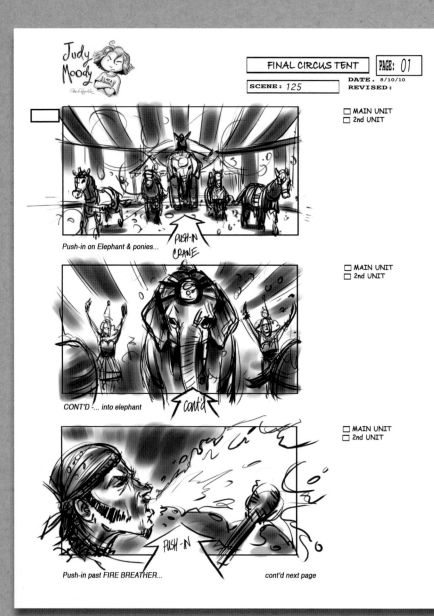

☐ MAIN UNIT
☐ 2nd UNIT

J S F Z BB's

OPAL, JUDY, STINK, FRANK
ZEKE, BIRNBAUMS

CRANE cont'd

Cont'd - PUSH-IN to our group...

☐ MAIN UNIT
☐ 2nd UNIT

cont'd

CONT'D -... push-in all the way to Judy

☐ MAIN UNIT
☐ 2nd UNIT

Angle on ponies / jugglers trotting past CAM

MOUSE, FELINE STARLET

The star feline on the set of *Judy Moody and the NOT Bummer Summer* is for sure and absolute positive . . . Mouse! This Moody cat has real stage presence, with an attitude certain to capture the attention of big studio executives. Mouse is waiting for her callback audition from famous director Steven Spielberg. Will she get the call?

JAWS, BOTANICAL SUPERSTAR

Jaws is Judy Moody's pet Venus flytrap. What was Jaws's favorite part of being on a movie set? Craft services, aka the food truck! Coming right up: burger (extra rare) and fresh flies—hold the ketchup!

In rehearsal

Ready and . . . action!

A flawless performance. Breathtaking!

Jaws is always on time and ready to perform.

No plants were harmed in the making of *Judy Moody and the NOT Bummer Summer*. Sadly, the same cannot be said about the flies.

Home, Sweet Home

117 Croaker Road
Frog Neck Lake, Virginia

Judy Moody and her family live in Virginia, the state of Pocahontas and Thomas Jefferson. Furthermore, they live in a town called Frog Neck Lake. (Oops! Sorry, Toady!)

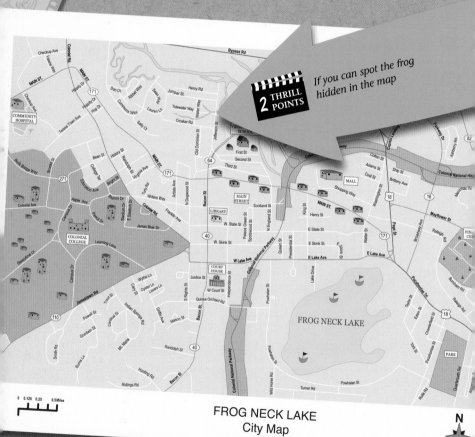

2 THRILL POINTS If you can spot the frog hidden in the map

FROG NECK LAKE
City Map

This map of Frog Neck Lake is based on a map of Williamsburg, Virginia, where Megan McDonald used to live!

The Moodys' movie house was in Studio City, California, more than two thousand miles away from Virginia!

Once the right house was found by the location scouts, it was painted to look spick-and-span for the movie. The house was made to look like a typical Virginia house, which meant that the front yard had to have oak trees (NOT palm trees). It also had to have enough space for a Bigfoot statue! Tons of roses in bloom added to the charm.

After

Before

Check out the pink front door! This house could win the Jessica Finch Seal of Approval.

The perfect Moody *backyard* was found in the town of South Pasadena, California—fifteen miles away from the perfect Moody *house*! It was chosen for its large, leafy trees—perfect for a backyard Bigfoot encounter!

After

Before

Aunt Opal was here!

A tree, a trap, a tent . . . and a whole lot of movie equipment and crew!

The only thing missing was the Moodys' backyard creek. Trying to find a babbling brook in Los Angeles in the summer was next to impossible. But that didn't stop the location manager, Kristi Frankenheimer. It took three days and some giant backhoes to make a realistic creek bed in the middle of the hot California desert. After the creek was filled with water, a truck-load of shrubs and trees was brought in to line the banks. *Voilà!* Instant Virginia creek.

A creek here?

Are you sure?

Presto change-o—a creek!

Watch out for toads!

WELCOME TO
FROG NECK LAKE, VIRGINIA

Judy Moody and the NOT Bummer Summer begins on the last day of school. When the final bell rings, kids pour out the door of San Rafael Elementary School, in Pasadena, California, which stood in for the Virginia Dare School.

School's out for summer! The colorful mural on the brick wall was painted just for the movie. What happened to it afterward? It stayed: a gift to SRES!

Virginia Dare School welcomes YOU!

The Glendora Village Pet Shop in the town of Glendora, California, was made to look like Fur & Fangs for the movie. Puppies, kittens, rabbits, guinea pigs, a parrot, and even a chinchilla became stars for a day.

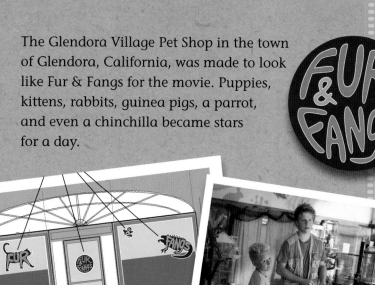

Turn to page 109. Can you spot this storefront in the background?

Stink stops in at Fur & Fangs to talk Bigfoot with Zeke.

Domenico's Jr. in Glendora was happy to pretend to be Gino's, the Moodys' favorite pizza joint. Sorry to say—they do not serve tuna-fish pizza, Stink's favorite, but they're happy to pile on the anchovies!

Waiting for the pizza

Pet store and pizza place graphics created by Teresa Keith

Judy and Frank try to score some thrill points on the Scream Monster roller coaster at Scare Devil Island. In fact, they are riding Goliath at Six Flags Magic Mountain in Valencia, California. This real-life rocket ship of a roller coaster will have you white-knuckling the safety bar in front of you until your hands are numb. Trust us: it's not for beginners! Built in 2000, Goliath is a steel hypercoaster that will have you hyperventilating just from looking at it. It combines a twister with an out-and-back layout. It once held world records for longest drop and top speed.

WARNING: Intense g-force may make you pull a Frank Pearl (aka upchuck!). Tip: Skip the blue cotton candy!

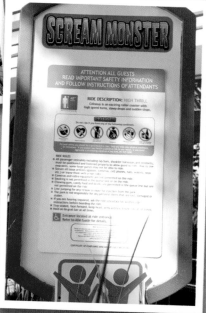

GOLIATH STATS:
- Height: 235 feet
- Angle of descent: 61°
- G-force: 4.5 g's (and we don't mean guinea pigs!)
- Drop: 255 feet
- Top speed: 85 mph

The Warner Grand Theatre is an old-fashioned movie house in San Pedro, California. It opened its doors on January 20, 1931. The owner nicknamed it the "Castle of Your Dreams," because it looks like an Art-Deco palace, complete with fancy ceilings and chandeliers. Add a host of wandering zombies, some mummies, and a mutant lobster, and it became the perfect place for Judy Moody and Frank Pearl to watch a Friday night Evil Creature Double Feature.

How do you turn a FUN Zone into an UN Zone? Knock off the letter F, of course. Find a spot by the water in San Pedro, California, and import some rusty old amusement park rides: one creaky Ferris wheel, two giant broken teacups, a few broken-down bumper cars. . . . Are we having UN-fun yet?

Larkspur Pier
Virginia's #1 Tourist
ATTRACTION

UN ZONE

Painting by Cynthia Charette

It was 113 degrees the day of filming—so hot that it broke the official Los Angeles city thermometer!

IN A TIGER-STRIPES MOOD
THE WRITERS TALK WITH
MARY JANE FORT, COSTUME DESIGNER

M&R: What was your favorite costume for the character of Judy Moody?

MJF: *I would have to say the Bride of Frankenstein! (see pages 86 and 132) I asked myself, "What would Judy do?" I thought she might rummage through her clothes and find an old purple tutu, so I started there.*

M&R: How do you start designing a wardrobe for a movie character?

MJF: *First, I try to get inside the character's head by reading the books and the screenplay. Then I visit real classrooms and look at what kids that age are wearing. I scour children's books and illustrations. I spend a lot of time thinking and trying to get the colors in my mind's eye. I look at European fashion, because often their fashion trends are ahead of the United States. Then I begin to sketch. . . .*

M&R: Did you have fun designing Aunt Opal's worldly costumes?

MJF: *From the minute you meet Opal, you want to know her. Her clothes give you an immediate sense of who she is. So in the first scene with Opal, I dressed her in cutoff shorts with blue boots, a crazy fur vest, a bright shoulder bag, and lots of accessories, including her signature armful of bangles and bracelets.*

M&R: What was another fun costume to make?

MJF: *Stink's berry-bush costume.*

M&R: What was the most difficult or challenging costume you had to design?

MJF: *That would be Judy's last-day-of-school tiger-striped pajama pants.* (see pages 14 and 83) *None of the animal prints I found looked right, so they had to be hand-designed and made. There are so many factors that went into making those pj's—printing techniques, the weight of the fabric, color passes trying to make them look worn rather than brand-new. All in all, the design took a few months to develop.*

ALL DRESSED UP

Using the personalities and interests of each character as her guide, Mary Jane Fort built a particular look, theme, or color range around each. For Rocky, it was hints of his circus roots. For Frank, it was all about preppy and plaid (and a little nerdy). Amy Namey had flower power. Jessica Finch, of course, couldn't get enough of pink. Zeke was the safari dude, and Stink was horizontal stripes, T-shirts with words, and some serious camo. Aunt Opal was fitted out with exotic textures, luxurious fabrics, jewel colors—a dazzling wardrobe collected from all corners of the world.

IN A BAD HAIR DAY MOOD

Costumes are step one in creating a character's look. Step two: hair and makeup. Some of the wildest dos? Judy's messy mop and moody curl, Stink's serious spikes, Zeke's parroty streaks, Mom's flippy wig, and Aunt Opal's wavy locks.

Wigged Out!

The kids on the set loved giving nicknames to everything, even the hairpieces!

- Janet's wig: Lynn Masters (after a famous Hollywood hairstylist)
- Heather's wigs: Nathalie and Natasha
- Heather's hair extensions: Nikita
- Taylar's hair extensions: Nana
- Jordana's Bride of Frankenstein wigs: Nancy and Nina
- Jordana's hairbrush: Nikki (Garrett wanted to name it Goblin.)

The curls attached to Jordana's hair each had a particular mood and personality, according to hairstylist Ramona Fleetwood. Jordana named them, of course: Ramona, Bobbi Sue, Nona, Hero Opal, and Navangelina for the blue-puke curl.

3 THRILL POINTS:

If you go to the movie *Judy Moody and the NOT Bummer Summer* dressed as Judy, Stink, Frank, Rocky, Amy, Jessica, Zeke, or Jessica Finch

+5 THRILL POINTS:

If you get your friends to do the same

JUDY "SCOOPS" MOODY TALKS TO

JM: Stink's favorite food is silver-dollar pancakes. What is your favorite?

PM: *My favorite food is steamed clams. Yum! I could eat them all day and night.*

JM: How old are you?

PM: *I'm eight.*

JM: Stink likes to read the *S* encyclopedia. How about you?

PM: *I read the Pokémon encyclopedia, but mostly I like inventing stuff. Like on set, the chairs don't have built-in tables. I want to invent the table chair. Another one is the Fan Shirt 3000. That's because it is so-o-o-o, so hot on set sometimes. I also invented a dice game about the Moodys. Especially Stink. It's called Scatters. It even has kitty litter in it!*

JM: Say no more. What do you like to do when you are not on set?

PM: *Swim. Especially in the ocean. I sometimes swim for a whole hour. A lot of days I swim for two miles.*

JM: Do you have any brothers or sisters?

PM: *In fact, I have four brothers. One older, three younger. NO sisters allowed!*

JM: How many pieces of hot dog did you have to eat or put in your mouth for the backyard fondue scene?

PM: *Gag me. You had to ask. It was over fifty. Oogley-boogley!*

PARRIS MOSTELLER (aka STINK)

In one shot, I have to spit out a hot-dog chunk. I spat it out and it landed on my arm and stuck there and we all cracked up. The director had to yell "Cut," he was laughing so hard.

JM: Did you ever enter your shoes in a smelly sneaker contest?

PM: *No, but I invented smell cups on set and sold them for a dollar each. There were all kinds of smells. Flowers. Tree bark. Dirt. Mint. Rose petals.*

JM: Sweet!

★ ★ 61 ★ ★

STINK'S FILM-O-PEDIA

Stink is a fact freak. He's also gaga over gadgets. So a movie set is like a dream come true for him. Here are just a few of the tidbits Stink, the human encyclopedia, picked up in Hollywood. Lights, camera, *fact*-ion!

"And CUT!": What the director calls out to end the filming of a scene; sound and film stop rolling.

"Background": The verbal signal to extras in a scene—such as a dog walker, a jogger, a shopper—to begin moving. This kind of detail makes the movie feel as if it could be taking place in real life.

Three extras stroll through a park. The one in the middle is the movie director's wife, Esther—for real!

Randy Johnson, boom operator, is dressed for a wet day at the office!

Boom: A long pole used to hold a microphone over the heads of the actors so that it won't show up on film. (The most common mistake in a movie is being able to spot a boom or its shadow in a scene!)

Checking the gate: If you spot someone peering into the wrong end of a camera lens, chances are he's "checking the gate:" making sure that no hair, lint, or other gunk has snuck inside. One always checks the gate before moving on to film a new scene. If the gate is dirty, the scene will need to be reshot.

Cherry picker: A crane that can hold a camera, a diffuser, a microphone, or other piece of equipment high and out of sight. Chances are you've seen telephone or electric workers use cherry pickers, too.

This cherry picker is holding a diffuser over the Moodys' backyard.

Lightbanks: An array of tools used to create and control light. They are often soft white boxes, called Chimeras, fitted over lights.

Clapboard: Also called the clapsticks or clapper, it contains information for each shot in a movie: title, director, scene number, date, time, etc. The clapping noise it makes is later used by editors to match up the sound with the picture.

Diffuser: Diffusers look a bit like big white sheets or canvasses, and are used to tone down sunlight or other bright lights. They come in different sizes and types.

Jim Leidholdt pushes the camera along the dolly tracks.

Dolly: A dolly is NOT a toy baby. It's a platform on wheels to which the camera can be attached. It's great for filming someone on the move, maybe riding a bike or running after Bigfoot!

End crawl: You know that long list of names in tiny type that comes at the end of a movie? That's called the end crawl.

Extras: Also called "background artists" or "background performers," extras are actors hired when a scene calls for large numbers or crowds of people. They don't usually have speaking lines.

Focus puller: Usually the first camera assistant (also known as the 1AC, and the person who heads up the camera department). Pulling focus means to measure the distance from the back of the camera lens to the subject being filmed. This measurement is used to get the camera focus just right.

Jorge Sanchez, 1AC, has his tape measure in hand, ready to pull focus.

Gaffer: The gaffer is the director of photography's right-hand person and is in charge of all lighting throughout the movie, indoors and out.

Grip: The job of the grip department is to cut, shape, and manipulate all light sources—electric or natural—based on the gaffer's instructions.

Balloon lights are used to lend a moonlit glow to a nighttime scene.

"It's a wrap!": That's what the director says when the last shot of the day has been completed and he or she is ready to go home and have dinner.

Magazine: A container loaded with film and attached to the movie camera. Usually very visible, as here with its red stripe.

"Picture's up!": This is what the production assistant announces to let everyone know that the cameras will soon be rolling. *Quiet down! Places, everyone!*

Director of photography Shawn Maurer's camera is fully loaded and ready to roll.

Process trailer: Cameras, sound equipment, producers, the script supervisor, and the director are piled onto this mini studio-on-wheels for shooting scenes on the go.

"Ready and . . . action!": When the director calls for "act-ion," the actors start saying their lines and, well, acting!

This process trailer is towing Humphrey, the Moody car, so that the camera can shoot straight into the car through the windshield.

Randall Stone, 2AC, lays down some stand Ts.

"Roll sound": The order to begin recording sound on the set.

Stand Ts: Colored markers on the ground that tell an actor or actress exactly where to stand for a scene. All actors and actresses are marked at all times with their own color, and the job of marking falls to the second camera assistant (2AC).

Steadicam: A camera that is worn by the camera operator with the help of a mechanical harness. The whole thing, often referred to as a rig, can weigh forty-five to fifty-five pounds! As the name suggests, it cuts down the amount of wobble or shake created by the camera operator's movements.

"Take 1, 2, 3 . . .": At the click of the clap-board, cameras are set to roll. The number of takes on the clapboard indicates how many times a scene has been filmed.

Jody Miller is both the steadicam operator and the A-Camera Operator.

Video Village: Video Village is where the producers, director, script supervisors, writers, and other crew gather to sit and watch the video monitors, which show the shot being filmed at that moment.

Walk and talk: Just what it sounds like! A scene in which the actors are being filmed as they are walking and talking. A steadicam or a camera mounted to a dolly might be used in a walk and talk.

The zeppelin was used during the crazy bicycle ride. Also pictured is a process trailer for camera and crew and a small process trailer for bike and riders!

Zeppelin: Looking a lot like a feather duster, a zeppelin is attached to a microphone to reduce the sound of air or wind. Great for action scenes in which the camera is moving at high speeds.

And that's a wrap!

Shawn Maurer preparing the camera for a scene featuring Janet Varney

Shawn Maurer with executive producer Andrew Sugerman

Shawn Maurer, DP

The director of photography (DP), or cinematographer, is the crew member who works most closely with the director during a film shoot. The director has the vision for how a scene should look, and it's up to the DP to pull together and manage the tools—cameras, lenses, filters, film stock, lighting—that will visually capture and then record that vision. This places the DP in charge of all camera operators, camera assistants, focus pullers, and lighting crews. It takes a lot of hard work, attention to detail, and experience to become a DP.

Judy "Scoops" Moody Talks to

If you've ever seen the TV show *Family Matters*, you may recognize "Mr. Todd" early in his acting career, at the age of twelve. Jaleel White, the actor who played Urkel on that show, is all grown up now. Judy Moody caught up with him on the set of *Judy Moody and the NOT Bummer Summer*.

JM: Mr. Todd is the World's Greatest Teacher. Who was *your* greatest teacher?

JW: *There were so many! I went to nine different schools throughout elementary and middle school.*

JM: If you had to pick just one, who would it be?

JW: *How about two? I have to credit Miss Thor, my seventh-grade English teacher, with teaching me how to construct sentences. But in fourth grade, I had the best teacher, Ms. McDonald. I was teacher's pet! I got straight A's that year, except for one U.*

JM: No way! U is for Unsatisfactory! Stink got one of those in gym. What subject did you get a U in?

JW: *Conduct!*

JM: What's conduct?

Jaleel White (aka Mr. Todd)

JW: *Conduct is how you behave in school. You get a U in it when you've been goofing off instead of studying!*

JM: Sweet! If you were in my class, you'd have to go to Antarctica to "chill out."

JW: *Don't forget: I am Mr. Todd. I invented Antarctica.*

"What I Did on My Summer Vacation"
by Mr. Todd

Have you ever wondered where your teachers go when the final bell rings on the last day of school? Well, it might surprise you to find out that we *don't* hang out in our classrooms all summer.

We catch up on hobbies

I grow a mean tomato, I love reading mysteries, and I like to hike. A friend of mine likes skydiving and bungee jumping!

We take classes

Some teachers take classes to learn about new subjects. That's right: when you're not in class, your teacher just might be. I'm thinking I'd like to learn how to play the didgeridoo. And I should brush up on my Italian before I take another trip to Bologna! There's always snake charming, too.

We travel

Teachers need vacations, too. A few of the places I'd like to visit: Patagonia, Australia, New Zealand, Antarctica, Mars.

We sleep in

Teachers like sleeping in on summer mornings almost as much as you do!

We get a summer job

One summer I worked at the Pickle Barrel deli making sandwiches. Another summer, I had a really *cool* job! (Hint: Watch the movie to find out what it was!) Maybe your teacher has a surprising summer job, too! Counting cheetahs in Africa?

Repairing coral reefs in the Bahamas? Brushing manatee teeth in Sarasota, Florida? Some other summer jobs teachers have held:

- waiter
- fishing guide
- professional singer
- soccer camp coach
- tour guide
- yoga instructor
- bookseller
- Segway rider
- yacht chef
- emergency medical technician
- dog walker
- house painter
- card dealer
- lifeguard

Look for *your* teacher at the mall, the park, the pool, or the public library.

5 THRILL POINTS If you find out what your teacher did last summer!

10 THRILL POINTS If you find out what Mr. Todd's summer job was in the movie!

JUDY "SCOOPS" MOODY TALKS TO

JM: Did you have to do anything special to prepare for the role of Rocky?

GR: *When I found out my character goes to circus camp, I went online and learned how to juggle.*

JM: What's your favorite magic trick?

GR: *The levitating salt trick. You pour a bunch of salt on the table. Then you balance the saltshaker on one edge, and it looks like it's floating.*

JM: What is your favorite scene in the movie?

GR: *The big good-bye scene at Rocky's house, because it's all about me—ha, ha! I got tossed upside down into Gilbert Grape (the car I drive off in with my mom).*

JM: Was it slimy to have to pick up a real toad in the creek?

GR: *Are you kidding? It was great! Toads are fun. There were actually three toads—a small, a medium, and a large—and they were all kind of squishy.*

JM: What do you like to do when you are not acting?

GR: *I love to read. Right now I'm reading* The Mysterious Benedict Society, *and it's awesome!*

JM: How old are you?

GR: *Eleven.*

GARRETT RYAN (aka ROCKY ZANG)

JM: Do you have any brothers or sisters?

GR: *Nope. I'm an only, so I'm in the Only Club with Ashley and Jordana. But I think it would be super-cool to have a big crazy family like Rocky's circus family.*

The Zang Family Circus

THE DAZZLING WHIZ-BANG ZANGS PRESENT

A CAVALCADE OF DELIGHTS AND DERRING-DO,

WHICH IS TO SAY,

AN ASTONISHING AND ENTIRELY SATISFYING ARRAY OF

MUSICAL, COMEDIC, ZOOLOGICAL, AND ACROBATIC

ENTERTAINMENT FOR LADIES, GENTLEMEN, YOUNG MISSES,

YOUNG MASTERS, AND EVEN THE LITTLE *BAMBINI*.

20 THRILL POINTS

If you put on your own backyard circus

That's a real elephant in the circus scene. But did Rocky really have to scoop the poop? Not exactly. The props department made balls of fake elephant poo, but they ran into a major pooper blooper! The poo was made of silicon (like rubber), so it bounced! They had to go back to the drawing board. It took four or five false starts, but finally . . . . *PLOPPPP!* No more poppy, peppy poop!

IN A SAME-SAME MOOD

On a movie set, stand-ins hold the place of actors while cameras and lighting are set up for a scene. A stand-in often has the same hair color, skin tone, and body type as his or her actor so that the lighting crew can get the lights just right. Stand-ins never appear on screen, but they are very important for a smooth film shoot.

Kimberly Throckmorten, stand-in for Judy, and Carla Watts, stand-in for Aunt Opal

By law, child actors are permitted to work for only a limited number of hours per day. Between takes, they study with their studio teachers. In the meantime, grown-ups who are about the same height as the kids stand in for them.

Kimberly Throckmorten and Tracey Thompson, stand-in for Stink

Kimberly Throckmorten and Frank Gieb, stand-in for Frank Pearl

Judy Moody has a famous elbow. Kasey Maline has a famous hand! Kasey was the photo double for Jordana. You might see her hand typing an e-mail or writing on the Thrill Points Chart.

Judy "Scoops" Moody Talks to

JM: What other movies have you been in, Taylar?

TH: *I just finished a movie called* Den Brother, *in which I play a girl named Abigail. It was fun because there were lots of kids and we filmed in Utah, where we got to experience snow. Not the snowman kind, the snowball kind.*

JM: Are you looking forward to being a member of the Toad Pee Club?

TH: *Ooh, ick! I have to let a real toad pee real pee on me! That is worth zero thrill points. But at least I get to wipe it off on you afterward. Hee, hee! Actually, that's my favorite scene in the movie.*

JM: Have you ever been to Borneo for real?

TH: *No. So far I've never left the United States. But someday I hope to go to Paris, France. I'm learning how to speak French right now. Ooh-la-la!*

JM: What do you like to do when you're not acting?

TH: *I'm on a dive team. And I love gymnastics and dance. Oh, and reading. Also, I love to cook. I like all the contraptions like cookie cutters, and I want to learn how to make croissants.*

JM: What's your favorite food?

TH: *Chicken and pasta.*

JM: What's your favorite pizza topping?

TH: *Does cheese count?*

TAYLAR HENDER (aka AMY NAMEY)

JM: What's your favorite color?

TH: *Pink and orange. I've always loved pink my whole life, but now orange is the new pink.*

JM: How are you like Amy Namey, the character you play?

TH: *I'm super organized. You should see Amy's suitcase! There are supposed to be ten Nancy Drew mysteries that she takes to Borneo, but there were only nine. (I counted.) By the way, I love Nancy Drew, too!*

JM: Same-same! If you were in charge of the Judy Moody movie sequel, what would it be about?

TH: *We would all go to Hawaii and swim with dolphins and ride a giant waterslide! No sharks allowed!*

JM: Rare!

Amy Namey's Video Diary

Dear Judy Most Moody,

Borneo is coolness! Never in a million years would you believe all the cool stuff here. I swam with (whale) sharks and fed a baby orangutan named Peaches. I'm having a swingin' good time. (Ha, ha, ha.)

WYWH (Wish You Were Here)

Ames

2 THRILL POINTS — If you can find Borneo on a map of the world

Peaches, banana, and me

How many thrill points is this worth?

★ ★ 80 ★ ★

Zip, zip, hooray!

Just hanging around

The Real Lost Tribe of Borneo
by Dr. E. Namey, PhD

The Penan people, sometimes referred to as a "lost tribe," are hunter-gatherers living in the rain forests of interior Borneo. They are noted for practicing *molong,* which means never taking more from their environment than necessary. The Penan are a generous, egalitarian people. Helping one another and working cooperatively is assumed, so much so that they have no word for *thank you* in their language. They don't need one. Logging and deforestation are now threatening the Penan way of life. Efforts are under way to block further destruction of their homeland.

Judy "Scoops" Moody Talks to

JM: Preston, how did you get into acting?

PB: *It was because my older brother, Brennan, is an actor. When I saw what he was doing, I realized that I wanted to do that, too. So I gave it a try.*

JM: Did you like dressing up as Frankenstein?

PB: *Totally! But trust me: it is not easy to walk or run down stairs in giant elevator shoes.*

JM: Do you have any ideas for a Judy Moody movie sequel?

PB: *I have two ideas. The first one would be that Judy, Frank, Rocky, and Amy build a time machine and then travel back or forward in time together. The second is that they would build a boat and then get stranded on an island with only a blanket to keep them warm.*

JM: How many times did you have to eat the T.P. Club meeting note in the school scene?

PB: *Seven, at least. And it didn't taste good. Bluck! It's like eating a pen or pencil.*

JM: What is your favorite scene in the movie?

PB: *Actually, there are two. I really like the theater scene with the zombies. And I like surfing in the beach scene just as much.*

JM: What do you like most about playing Frank "Eats Paste" Pearl?

PRESTON BAILEY (aka FRANK PEARL)

PB: *I like the fact that I finally get to be in a movie that's for kids. See, in the other shows or movies I've been in, I play a kid but the movie is for grown-ups.*

JM: What is your favorite pizza topping?

PB: *Cheese is my favorite. But guess what? Once I had a pizza when I was on a movie set in Hungary and it had corn and steak for toppings.*

"How to Ride a Roller Coaster without Spewing"

by Frank Pearl

1. **Sit toward the front.** The farther back you sit, the faster you—and your stomach—drop after a steep climb!

2. **On a corkscrew coaster, sit toward the back** so you can see what's coming. (If the people in front of you live through the turn, chances are, you will, too).

3. **Don't ride right after pigging out.** (Or at least eat foods that won't turn your friends blue when you throw up on them.)

4. **Try not to imagine falling out of your seat and going SPLAT,** like an overripe melon, on the ground below. Roller coasters are safety-inspected every single day.

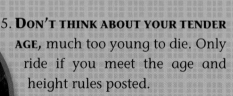

5. **Don't think about your tender age,** much too young to die. Only ride if you meet the age and height rules posted.

6. **Scream.** A lot if you need to. Really—it helps!

JUDY MOODY GETS THE BLUES!

CLICK-CLICK-CLICK-CLICK-CLICK. How would you like to be ascending a 235-foot, straight-up steep hill, trying to remember your lines, thinking about your facial expressions, keeping your eyes open the whole time, with three cameras only inches from your face, and know that any second you are going to be covered in flying blue puke? That's what Jordana Beatty, aka Judy Moody, had to do in the roller-coaster scene. No, that's not a stunt double! What was the blue puke made of? Vanilla pudding! Add a blueberry granola bar, oatmeal, Rice Krispies, blue Jell-O, and—*voilà!*—Puke Monster!

2 THRILL POINTS If you've ridden a roller coaster at least once in your life

5 THRILL POINTS If you've ridden a corkscrew roller coaster with your eyes open!

Megan McDonald checks Jordana's reaction to watching herself turn blue on the roller coaster!

ARE YOU A FUN SPONGE?

"You're nothing but one big wet . . . FUN SPONGE!"

A fun sponge is someone who's in a bad mood and sucks the fun out of everything. Take this quiz and find out where you rate on the Sponge-O-Meter.

WOULD YOU RATHER:
A. Go to circus camp?
B. Take a trip to Borneo?
C. Take your stuffed animals to obedience school?

WOULD YOU RATHER:
A. Sit through a whole entire scary movie?
B. Ride a roller coaster all day?
C. Count socks in a drawer?

WOULD YOU RATHER:
A. Make a giant hat out of a garbage-can lid?
B. Make a thrill-o-delic Thrill Points Chart?
C. Rake leaves all day without jumping in the pile?

WOULD YOU RATHER:
A. Go on a midnight stakeout?
B. Make up secret code words for your walkie-talkies?
C. Not share your night-vision goggles with anyone?

WOULD YOU RATHER:
A. Learn to walk on a tightrope?
B. Walk to Fur & Fangs?
C. Not walk to meet your friend for ice cream at Screamin' Mimi's?

WOULD YOU RATHER:
A. Catch a South American marine toad?
B. Catch a super-fast fly ball?
C. Catch a cold and stay in bed all day?

WOULD YOU RATHER:
A. Teach your cat to make toast?
B. Teach your guinea pig to do yoga?
C. Babysit a pet rock?

THRILL POINTS

Turn to page 136 to earn thrill points and find out if you're a fun sponge!

Judy "Scoops" Moody Talks to

JM: How long have you been an actress?

HG: *I've been acting since I was a teenager. Some of my first movie roles were in* Drugstore Cowboy *and* License to Drive.

JM: That's so funny that your first movie was about a kid who flunked his driving test and can't really drive. And now you have to play my aunt, who is a terrible driver!

HG: *I know!*

JM: Where did you grow up?

HG: *I grew up in Virginia.*

JM: Same-same!

HG: *My dad was in the FBI (top secret!), and my mom was a teacher. She also wrote children's books.*

JM: Cool beans! What stuff did you like to do when you were my age?

HG: *I'm a reader, and I was* way *into Pippi Longstocking. I love how she has special powers.*

JM: I know. She has super-human strength! I wish I could lift a horse one-handed.

HG: *I know, right?*

JM: What do you like to do when you're not acting?

HG: *I am way into yoga.*

HEATHER GRAHAM (aka AUNT OPAL)

JM: Hold the phone! I like yoga-not-yogurt, too. I even taught Mouse the cat some yoga poses.

HG: *I think we're a lot alike. I also like dance, cooking and eating with friends, swimming in the ocean, and scuba diving.*

JM: I heard it was your idea to do the freeze dance in the movie. That is so way cool.

HG: *And thrill-a-delic.*

JM: You seem to love music. What are you listening to right now?

HG: *Radiohead, lots of world and alternative music. I like to choose a song before my scene that helps me get into character and fits with the tone and mood of the scene.*

JM: What are you listening to today?

HG: *I've been listening to "Free" a lot, by Ultra Nate.*

JM: What did you like about the character of Aunt Opal that made you want to take the role?

HG: *I love Opal's backstory—I find the character of Aunt Opal so interesting; that she's been to art school in Berlin and traveled the world doing guerrilla art. She gets to burst onto the Moody scene, making an immediate connection with Judy and Stink, and it's just so sweet and funny and magical, like a contemporary Mary Poppins.*

IN AN OPALIZING MOOD

Judy Moody's Aunt Awful arrives with not just another suit-case—but a super-duper gigantic trunk! Inside is a travel-ing art studio full of paints and brushes and ribbons and stickers and beads and . . . tons more stuff for making art.

After much searching, the perfect trunk for Aunt Opal was found. It's an old, antique trunk from the Metropolitan Opera House, in New York City. One look and you just know this trunk has a history. Valerie Green, art director, spent *hours* getting the trunk gorgeously outfitted for the movie.

It belonged to a famous opera singer named Dorothy Kirsten. Kirsten, a soprano, got her start at the Metropolitan Opera singing in the role of Mimi in *La Bohème,* in 1945, and sang at the Met for the next thirty years, becoming famous for roles in *Tosca* and *Madame Butterfly.* She also starred in movies and has a star on the Hollywood Walk of Fame.

Aunt Opal's trunk of wonders

Aunt Opal is a guerrilla-not-gorilla artist. That means she makes art out of everything and puts it everywhere.

Beauty creates the Beast

Judy tries her hand at guerrilla art, too.

Garbage-can lids never looked so good!

Art, anyone?

Magical!

Set dressers make messes look great!

MOVIE MAGIC

It took a lot of artists and designers to create Judy Moody's world. From backyard to bunk bed, from park to pier, from Scream Monster to Scream Fest, it all began with reading the books and poring over the drawings. After reading the script many times over, the production designer, Cynthia Charette, began to see the geography of Judy Moody's world in her mind's eye.

With leaps of imagination, not to mention heaps of color, fabric, wallpaper, paint, artists, and craftspeople, and countless meetings and discussions with Valerie Green, art director; Don Diers, set decorator; and Mary Jane Fort, costume designer, Judy's world sprang to life.

Cynthia Charette, production designer, and Don Diers, set decorator

"The Cave": Meeting place for the
Bigfoot Believer's Association

Inside the T.P. Club tent

Amy Namey's room

A moonlit midnight stakeout

Stink's room, complete with car bed and "Stink 3000" wallpaper!

The Moodys' stairwell, a gallery that includes real baby pictures of Jordana and Parris

The Moodys' kitchen is sunny, warm, and welcoming.

The wallpaper in Judy's room was custom-made to echo the curl on the top of her head. But that's not the only place Cynthia Charette used the swirly curl shape to decorate something! She used it 61 times!

Cynthia Charette and Darwin Browne, key grip

THRILL POINT For every swirly curl shape you spot in the movie!

Hint: chances are not all 61 will be visible in the final film. Do your best!

The property master's job is to find or make any objects needed in the film. In this case, Tom Cahill had to supervise the making of a giant jellyfish, poop, and puke, among other things.

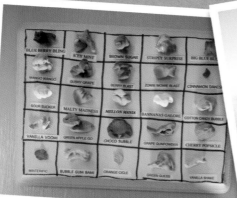

Judy's ABC gum collection

Tom Cahill displays some of his team's handiwork.

Dozens of Thrill Point charts were made for the movie.

Check out that tiger-striped seat!

The poop in the sandwiches Judy, Stink, and Aunt Opal take on their picnic was made of chocolate fondant with cranberries and rasperries. It may LOOK like scat, but it tasted like a candy bar. Yummmm!

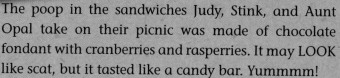

Kenneth Garrett sculpted this elephant head. Watch out below!

Bench by Aunt Opal (but not really)! Chuck Coffman was master installer and artist on this masterpiece.

Between the art, design, property, and construction teams, there were more than forty people involved in the creation of the places and things seen in *Judy Moody and the NOT Bummer Summer.*

THE BIGFOOT STATUE

A Styrofoam block, old rugs, Spanish moss, palm fronds, duct tape, tree bark . . . add some baseball eyes and *voilà!* Bigfoot lives! Fifty cents a touch!

Bigfoot by Kenneth Garrett, sculptor, and Chuck Coffman, key fabricator

Judy "Scoops" Moody Talks to

JM: What was the best part about playing Zeke? Was it that my little "bother," Stink, really looked up to you and thought you were way cool?

JO: *I just love playing a character who's the opposite of me, I mean, this guy is so totally into Bigfoot, it's crazy. Also, the hairspray.*

JM: Is it true that you are a brainiac? Stink says you are trying to join some super-genius Einstein club named Mental or something?

JO: *It's called Mensa. You have to have a super-high IQ, and I'm off by only three points. So if you have any tips on how to get smarter fast, let me know. I'm thinking about that sleeping-on-the-dictionary thing that worked for you—when all those big vocabulary words went into your brain.*

JM: Speaking of being a genius, do you go to regular school and have a teacher like Mr. Todd? What kind of things do you like to study?

JO: *I'm home-schooled, so my teacher is pretty much my mom. Right now, I'm interested in astrophysics, so I read up on that a lot in my spare time.*

JM: At the opening cast party, I heard you singing. Is that something you do a lot of when you are not acting? Maybe you and I should sing "On Top of Spaghetti" to drive Stink crazy!

JACKSON ODELL (aka ZEKE)

JO: *I am way into music. I play piano, drums, bass, and guitar. I sang in a choir when I was your age. I got into music from my older brother—I have 11,000 songs on my computer: John Mayer, Eric Clapton, Led Zeppelin, Jimi Hendrix, B.B. King.*

JM: Did you grow up in Hollywood, or can you tell your fans where you're from?

JO: *I'm from Colorado, but I hang out in Los Angeles a lot when I'm filming a TV show or movie. You might have seen me on an episode of* Modern Family.

JM: Are you even old enough to drive a Vespa?

JO: *I'm only thirteen, so I don't have a driver's license for real. But in the movie I do!*

NO ANIMALS WERE HARMED IN THE MAKING OF THIS FILM.

Have you ever wondered where that phrase comes from? The Film & TV Unit of the American Humane Association, which monitors animal treatment on more than one thousand productions every year, makes sure that animals used in movies and on TV are happy and healthy on set. They make sure that any animal actors don't work too many hours, have good and comfortable places to live, interact well with their human and animal costars, and even if and how they can wear costumes.

The blue and yellow macaw at Fur & Fangs is a parrot named Rainbow. Macaws make great pets because of their beauty and their ability to talk. They eat seeds, nuts, fruits and vegetables, and especially enjoy pasta! *Spaghetti, anyone?*

The movie star Mouse is played by two honest-to-meow Hollywood working cats. Their names are Tux and Tails. No lie. According to Shawn Weber and Sheri Aparicio, the animal trainers and handlers, Tux is the stunt cat, and Tails is the true actor. You decide if you can spot the difference. *High five, Mouse!*

Three toads—Freddy, Ernest, and Hemingway—were used in the movie. All three are South American marine toads, also known as cane toads or giant toads. In Belize, they're even called spring chickens! *Croak, croak, cluck!*

Nugget is the name of the opossum that appears in the nighttime stakeout scene. Nugget may be afraid of Bigfoot, because she did not want to come out and swing from a tree that night. Can you blame her? Scarrryyyy!

Five talented dogs were rescued from an animal shelter: Jessie, Zoe, Bobby, Harlan, and Austin. After lots of training, these are the doggies you'll see chasing Bigfoot down Croaker Road (Judy Moody's street).

Those talented ponies at the circus are no robots! They are the very real Silver, Sassy, Charlie, and Rocky (Hey, same-same!).

Susie is a very sweet, very big twenty-five-year-old African elephant.

HONK IF YOU'RE MOODY

What does YOUR race-car bed say? Make a statement with bumper stickers.

Stink's got them on his bed. Zeke sports them on his Vespa. And the Birnbaums can be quoted: "Say it with a slogan."

got bigfoot?

Bumper stickers created by Teresa Keith and Lauren Day

2 THRILL POINTS If you make your own Bigfoot bumper sticker

Life is Short: Believe in Bigfoot

I BRAKE FOR... BIGFOOT

Take a Peek at Zeke's Vespa

When Zeke has to get somewhere fast, like to Fur & Fangs or a Bigfoot Believers meeting, what better way to travel than on his sleek, shiny black Vespa? Keep a sharp eye out in the movie for someone else who might take a late-night ride on this dash-about-town scooter. If you think it's Bigfoot—think again!

"Good luck, little dude. You, too, Moody Girl. Call me if you see anything. Day or night."

So You Want to Catch Bigfoot?

Camouflage netting, night-vision goggles, camcorder, whistles, coffee (blech!). Everything you need for a Bigfoot emergency. Need backup? The Birnbaums' van is at your service.

The Birnbaums' van was fitted out by Chuck Coffman, key fabricator

So You Want to Catch **BIGFOOT?**

As Seen in the Film
Judy Moody AND THE NOT BUMMER SUMMER

Any Bigfooter worth his salt should read Dr. Morgan Jackson's book, *So You Want to Catch Bigfoot?* He gives lots of good tips and advice, and the Birnbaums own multiple copies. Here's just a sample from this essential volume:

THE STAKEOUT: PACK YOUR BAGS

Poor preparation could lead to a hair-raising situation. First gather the necessary supplies and Bigfoot-catching equipment. Triple-check to make sure you didn't forget anything.

THINGS YOU'LL NEED:

- Camouflage netting
- Night-vision goggles
- Tent
- Sleeping bag
- Binoculars
- Emergency sirens
- Whistles
- Nose clip (a Bigfoot's smell has caused some to pass out.)
- Camcorder with night vision
- TWO cameras with night vision (an extra for backup)
- Tape recorders
- Tape of vocalizations (optional)
- Supplies for building a trap
- Supplies for gathering evidence: latex gloves, tongs, tweezers, plastic bag, marker for labeling specimens
- TWO coolers—one for food and one for scat (Careful not to mix these up!)
- Journal for recording data
- Equipment for making casts of footprints
- Tranquilizer gun
- Flashlight
- Protective metallic suit
- Disguise and/or camouflage gear
- Meals, eating utensils, a thermos, and lots of coffee or hot chocolate
- *So You Want to Catch Bigfoot?* (the book!)

5 THRILL POINTS If you read So You Want to Catch Bigfoot?

The Peanut-Butter Trap

Bigfoot is nuts about peanut butter, making this a trap it can't resist. How it works in a nutshell: A net is hung from a tree. Peanut-butter jars are attached to the net. When Bigfoot yanks on a jar, the net falls on it, and—wham!—you've snagged your first Sasquatch.

What You'll Need:

- 30 jars of peanut butter
- 30 pieces of string (3 feet each)
- Net or hammock
- Old hooded sweatshirt (large)
- Old baseball cap
- Glue
- Leaves
- Twigs
- Berries (Any berries will do.)

Total camo!

1. Create a berry-bush disguise. Glue leaves, twigs, and berries onto the sweatshirt and cap. Set aside.

2. Hang a large net from various branches of a tree. Make sure the netting is hidden among the leaves and not in sight.

3. Tie thirty peanut-butter jars to the netting. They should dangle low enough for Bigfoot to see and reach.

4. Put on your disguise.

5. Hide and wait.

LETTING BIGFOOT GO

Untie several jars of peanut butter from the net and quickly roll them over to Bigfoot. While it's distracted by the peanut butter, slowly begin pulling the net off and throw more jars as far as you can into the woods. Bigfoot will chase the jars, not you.

Flashlight? Check. Camouflage netting? Check. Night-vision goggles? Check. Walkie-talkies? Check. No sleeping, no snoring. Check. And now the wait. What was that? Stink? Did you hear that? Do you think it's—

CODE RED! CODE RED! BIGGGGGFOOOOOTTTTT!

The trap has been set!

20 THRILL POINTS For having your own Bigfoot stakeout!

The Bigfoot stakeout has officially begun.

Judy and Stink tiptoed farther and farther into the gloom.

"Holy macaroni! It's . . . it's him!"

ICE CREAM AND BAND-AIDS

As a child, Megan McDonald grabbed a dime, ran down the street, and chased after the ice-cream truck nearly every day of summer. One day, it took forever to find a dime, so she had to run up a steep hill to try to catch the truck on the next street. *Crash! Bang! OOPS!* She fell down the hill and had to get twelve stitches. Ouch! That's one big Band-Aid and no ice cream. Her experience inspired the ice-cream truck chase in *Judy Moody and the NOT Bummer Summer.*

HOLD FOR FILE

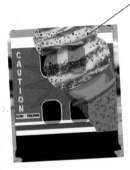

Benjamin Moore Colors

2078-30
Royal Fuscia

2079-40
Springtime Bloom

OC-122
Cotton Balls

2060-30
Seaport Blue

OC-66
Snow White

Turn to page 34 for a look at the real truck.

IN A FAKE-O BRAND MOOD

While the town of Frog Neck Lake is based, loosely, on Williamsburg, Virginia, it is not an actual place you can find on any real map. To give it a sense of being real-but-not-real, just about everything was made up and given a name by Megan McDonald herself, including products, places, street names, bumper stickers, and labels.

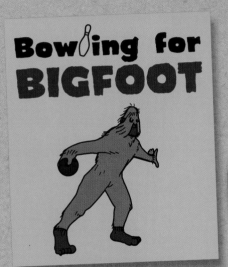

Bobbi Sue's PUPPY CHOW

"Because your puppy deserves the best."

Can you figure out which movie VIP this chow is named for?

This brand name came from a Peter H. Reynolds illustration in Judy Moody Saves the World!

CONK Peanut Butter

257

TAXI SHIFT 2 GREEN
— FROG NECK LAKE, VA —

ADOPT A HERMIT CRAB!

Megan McDonald also wrote a book about a hermit crab!

The Mermaid's Toenail

20 30 40 50 60 70 80 °F
BRRR CHILLY BRISK SO-SO WARM
FROSTY 0°C 10 20
FREEZING -10 -20
0 -10 -20 °F

LOOK OUT!!! IT'S GETTING HOT IN HERE!

FROSTY FREEZER
HARDWARE
MADE IN FROG NECK LAKE, VA

7 WH2O NEWS

PASSENGER'S SIDE

"3-D Me"

by Judy Moody

Most of the *NOT Bummer Summer* movie is live action, which means real kids and people act the parts. But there are a few places where you get to see what's inside my imagination! These scenes are done in 3-D animation by a company called Reel FX. They are super, way-cool famous for working on movies like *Bee Movie, Kung Fu Panda,* and *Open Season 2* and *3*!

And now they've turned me, Judy Moody, into a cartoon. They start out with a flat drawing of me from the Judy Moody books. Then they make a model of me on the computer. Next, they add movement, and before you know it, the cartoon me can walk across a tightrope! Magic! And guess what else? I *finally* have eyes, not just dots! I can blink! YAY!

Watch me go from this . . .

Fasten your seat belts! You won't believe *your* eyes when I go to Antarctica, cross the great Niagara Falls on a tightrope, or saw my best friend Rocky in half! Hardee-har-har! Even Mouse might have to close her eyes!

to THIS!

Judy "Scoops" Moody Talks to

JM: Ashley, you play the character of Jessica Finch in the movie version of my life. What do you and Jessica Finch have in common?

AB: *We both love pigs!*

JM: What's your favorite color?

AB: *Pink, of course! Same-same as Jessica Finch.*

JM: Are you an excellent speller like Jessica Finch?

AB: *I wish I could say yes, but not really. But I can spell HIPPOPONAMUS. (Look it up. See if I'm right.)*

JM: I know Jessica Finch would like to be in the Toad Pee Club. Are you in any clubs?

AB: *Yep! I'm in the Peegie Weegie Club. Anybody who can say Peegie Weegie can be in the club. (I would not want to be in the Gross Grub Club, even if you gave me a real-live potbelly pig.)*

JM: How old are you?

AB: *I just turned ten, so that puts me in the Double Digits Club, too. Ha!*

JM: Do you have any brothers or sisters?

AB: *Nope. I'm an only, and, yep, that's another club I'm in.*

JM: What do you like most about playing Jessica Finch?

AB: *The last character I played was a good girl. I like playing a character that does not have to be super-nice all the time.*

Ashley Boettcher (aka Jessica Finch)

JM: Do you have an idea for another Judy Moody movie?

AB: *You read my mind! In the next movie, Judy Moody and Jessica Finch should be zapped with a brain transplant. They just wake up one day, and—bam!—Jessica Finch's brain would be in Judy Moody's body and vice versa. It would be so funny and way confusing and mix everybody up.*

JM: Whoa!

Jessica's bike was decorated behind the scenes by Aimee O'Shea.

JESSICA FINCH'S MOVIE REVIEW

Judy Moody and the NOT Bummer Summer movie is a must-see, way-funny movie for kids and families. It is SO not just for girls. Boys are gonna love all the crazy action and comedy. Hardee-har-har! The roller coaster scene alone is worth the price of admission. I am N-O-T kidding. My favorite part is, of course, when I, Jessica Finch, get to ride the pink piggy bike and go faster than Humphrey, the Moody car. My UN-favorite part is that there are NO real-live PIGS in this movie, because I love-love-love pigs. (Even if there is a cat, a toad, an opossum, a macaw, four ponies, and an elephant.) Just wait for the sequel! And guess what—I am STILL not in the Toad Pee Club! No fair! Would someone PUH-LEASE talk to the writers? But don't be an aardwolf—go see this movie anyway! In a word, it's H-I-L-A-R-I-O-U-S! On a scale of 1 to 5, I give this movie **5 oinks!!**

OINK! OINK! OINK! OINK! OINK!

"THERE ARE NO SMALL PARTS, ONLY SMALL ACTORS"

by Jessica Finch

I'm on screen for all of like three seconds. Doesn't seem like much, right? But think about it: if I hadn't been riding by on my bike at just the right moment, Judy and her aunt would never have been able to swipe it and use it to catch up with the ice-cream truck. If they hadn't been able to catch up to the ice-cream truck, the movie's key mysteries would never be solved! See what I mean? The point is, every single person is crucial to the success of the movie. Without me, the entire movie would have wobbled and fallen apart.

AND THE WINNER OF THE GIRAFFE AWARD IS . . .

Sarah Siegel-Magness! She is the Queen of Green. Sarah made the set of *Judy Moody and the NOT Bummer Summer* an earth-friendly one. Everyone even got their own reusable water bottle. How green was the Judy Moody set? I, Judy Moody, Garbologist, was on the case. Here's my way-official report. Check out all the stuff that got recycled in just *one* week on set! Not one single piece of garbage was sent to a landfill. Now that's *uber*-rare! No lie.

How much was recycled in one week?

- Bottles and cans: 72 pounds
- Cardboard: 231 pounds
- Paper: 61 pounds
- Compost (like ooey-gooey banana peels): 2180 pounds
- Metal: 64 pounds
- Green waste: 74 pounds

HELP HEAL THE WORLD!

The Environmental Media Association (EMA) has made it their mission to get folks in the entertainment industry to work in a more earth-friendly way. How? By giving out awards to the greenest of the green: actors, directors, studios, production companies, you name it.

Winners are announced at a special banquet every year. Doesn't that make you feel green with envy? At the awards banquet, organic food and drinks are served on chinaware (not paper or plastic!), reusable cloth banners and signs are used, and all paper materials are printed using soy-based ink on 100-percent recycled chlorine-free paper. And, of course, as much as possible is recycled.

> *"Never doubt that a small group of concerned people can change the world."*
>
> **—Margaret Mead**

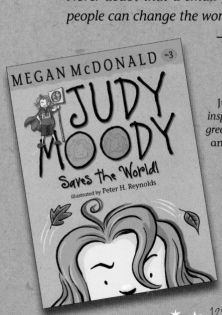

Judy Moody Saves the World! *inspired Sarah Siegel-Magness to go green for the filming of* Judy Moody and the NOT Bummer Summer!

An Album

Hunter; Werewolf:
Cameron Boyce

WH2O Newscaster:
Jenn Korbee

Scream Monster ticket taker:
Pedro Shanahan

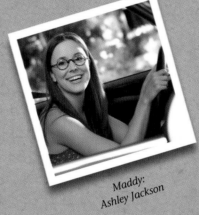

Maddy:
Ashley Jackson

Rocky's mom:
Jenica Bergere

Derrick, the surf instructor:
Frank Caronna

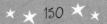

Movie ticket seller:
Norwood Cheek

Screaming woman
(AND executive producer!):
Bobbi Sue Luther

Rod Serling–type narrator:
James McManus

Zombie tourist:
Brian Palermo

Ivy, the movie ticket taker:
Megan Franich

Ringmaster:
Richard Riehle

John Schultz (center) confers with Richard Gibbs, composer (left), and Hal Olofsson (right), first assistant director.

Smile, Mrs. Frankenstein!

Stunt coordinator Joel Kramer with a couple of soggy actors

Jordana and Garrett show off their summer T-shirts.

Richard Haynes and Megan McDonald consult with Steve Gehrke, script supervisor.

Zombies like going to the movies, too.

Members of the Flip Club:
Taylar, Garrett, Cameron,
Preston, and Ashley

Animal handler
Shawn Webber
coaches Tux. Or
is that Tails?

John Schultz and Jody
Miller get in nice and
close for the scream!

Garrett Ryan with
Bobbi Sue Luther,
executive producer

John, is that you?

Kristoffer Winters and Janet Varney (aka Dad and Mom) ham it up.

Jordana and production assistant John Pace IV eye the surf.

Producer Sarah Siegel-Magness tries on Jody Miller's rig for size.

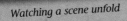

Watching a scene unfold

Eeeew! Is that ABC gum?

Parris gets Opalized!

Megan, Garrett, and Preston chat between takes.

"It's a wrap!"

Answer Key

Answers from page 26

1. Mom
2. Dad
3. Dad
4. Mom
5. Mom
6. Mom
7. Dad
8. Dad

Answers from page 87

For each A answer, score 3
For each B answer, score 2
For each C answer, score 1

Add them all up. If you score 15–21, you are NOT a Fun Sponge. Five thrill points to you!

If you score 10–14, you are heading in the right direction but can sometimes be a Fun Rag or Fun Sponge.
Two thrill points for trying.

If you score less than 10, sorry, you are a Fun Mop! Subtract 3 thrill points!

(Don't forget to add your final total to your thrill points chart.)

SELECTED SOURCES

Stink's Film-O-Pedia
(pages 62–67)

http://www.filmsite.org/filmterms.html
http://www.imdb.com/glossary/

In a Same-Same Mood
(pages 76–77)

http://standincentral.com/2010/04/
   28/interview-with-sarah-brynne/

No Animals Were Harmed
in the Making of this Film.
(pages 104–107)

http://www.americanhumane.org/
   protecting-animals/programs/
   no-animals-were-harmed/legacy-
   of-protection.html

http://www.slate.com/id/2117565/

So You Want to Catch Bigfoot?
(pages 110–111)

Excerpt from *So You Want to Catch Bigfoot?* by
Morgan Jackson with Jamie Michalak, illustrated
by Mark Fearing (Candlewick Press, 2011).

"3-D Me" by Judy Moody
(pages 122–123)

http://www.radiumreelfx.com/entertainment

ACKNOWLEDGMENTS

The author and editor are grateful to the many people who so generously and patiently shared their time, energy, resources, and knowledge so that Judy Moody fans could take an amazing journey behind the scenes of *Judy Moody and the NOT Bummer Summer.* A very special thank-you to Sarah Siegel-Magness for saying "Yes" and and for saying "Welcome." Double high fives to the *uber*-awesome Bobbi Sue Luther, Richard Haynes, and Suzanne Tenner, who all went WAY above and beyond. Mega-thanks to Cynthia Charette, Don Diers, Mary Jane Fort, Tom Cahill, and Ben White for sharing their expertise and their enthusiasm.

It took an entire team of people to work on this and all of the Judy Moody movie tie-in books at Candlewick Press, but a special shout-out to Kristen Nobles, Lisa Rudden, and Liz Zembruski, as well as to Sally Bratcher, Maggie Deslaurier, Angela Dombroski, Martha Dwyer, Kate Fletcher, Gregg Hammerquist, Becky Hemperly, Kim Lanza, Karen Lotz, Hannah Mahoney, Mary McCagg, Heather McGee, Joan Powers, Peter H. Reynolds, Julianna Rose, Rachel Smith, Ann Stott, and Katie Warren.

PHOTO AND ILLUSTRATION CREDITS

All the photographs in this book were taken by Suzanne Tenner, set photographer, with the following exceptions:

Pages 10–13: professional head shots (center column of images) provided by Smokewood Entertainment

Pages 14, 112, 129, 137, and 142–143: book covers courtesy of Candlewick Press

Page 24: photo of Megan McDonald, Jordana Beatty, and Peter H. Reynolds courtesy of Smokewood Entertainment, taken by Nick Snyder

Pages 34–37: storyboards courtesy of Smokewood Entertainment, drawn by James Doh and Rod Douglas

Page 40: map of Frog Neck Lake courtesy of Smokewood Entertainment, designed by Lauren Day

Pages 41–43: house and creek location shots courtesy of Smokewood Entertainment, taken by Valerie Green and Kristi Frankenheimer

Pages 45, 48, 108, 118–121: logos, storefront designs, bumper stickers, and vehicle detail courtesy of Smokewood Entertainment

Page 48: painting of Larkspur Pier courtesy of Smokewood Entertainment, created by Cynthia Charette

Pages 80–81: Amy Namey's Video Diary images courtesy of Smokewood Entertainment, created by Lauren Day

Pages 123 and 137: animation cel courtesy of Smokewood Entertainment, created by Reel FX

Judy Moody and the NOT Bummer Summer

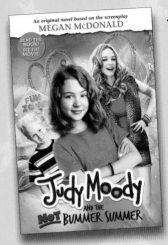

Roar! Just when it looks like Judy Moody's summer is going to be BOR-ing—eureka!—she comes up with the most thrill-a-delic plan ever. Get ready for a race involving tightropes, roller coasters, and zombies! Add in a hunt for Judy's teacher, an *uber*-adventurous aunt, a midnight stakeout, a runaway ice-cream truck, and a dash of Bigfoot, and what have you got? The Judy Moodiest summer ever!

By Megan McDonald, based on the screenplay
by Kathy Waugh and Megan McDonald.
Features full-color stills from the movie

So You Want to Catch Bigfoot?

Stink is on high alert when several sightings of Bigfoot have been made in the neighborhood. To assist him in his search for the elusive creature, Aunt Opal gives Stink a copy of *So You Want to Catch Bigfoot?* Now Judy Moody and Bigfoot fans alike can own a facsimile of this valuable field guide, containing everything you need to know about the furry fugitive, including tips on trapping and releasing your specimen.

by Morgan Jackson PhD
with Jamie Michalak,
illustrated in black and
white by Mark Fearing

Judy Moody and the Thrill Points Race

Judy Moody is psyched for summer—that is, until she realizes that two of her three best friends aren't going to be around: Rocky will be teaching lions to jump through hoops at circus camp, and Amy is going to be searching for lost tribes in the rain forests of Borneo. How can Judy's summer ever compare? But she is determined that her summer will NOT be a bummer, that she and Frank Pearl will have the most NOT bummer summer ever—with plenty of thrill points to prove it!

by Jamie Michalak,
illustrated in full color with movie stills and original photographs taken on the set

by Jamie Michalak,
illustrated in full color with movie stills and original photographs taken on the set

Judy Moody and the Poop Picnic

Judy is desperately trying to earn thrill points, so she plans a trip to the Cemetery Creep 'n' Crawl. Meanwhile, Stink has been collecting all the samples and evidence he can in his efforts to catch Bigfoot. Add in Aunt Opal's crazy driving (and bad sense of direction), and somehow they all end up at an abandoned amusement park, eating scat sandwiches. That's gotta be worth some thrill points. . . .

Need more Moody?

Celebrating 10 mega-

Try these!

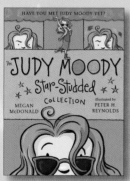

Moody years. No lie!

★ ★ ★ Your Thrill Points! ★ ★ ★

Page #	Challenge	Possible Points	Your Points
25	Tongue Twister 1	3	
25	Tongue Twister 2	6	
26	Moody Squared	8	
27	Do Not Disturb	10	
33	John Schultz Movies	6	
40	Frog Neck Lake	2	
59	Bad Hair Day 1	3	
59	Bad Hair Day 2	5	
71	Summer Jobs 1	5	
71	Summer Jobs 2	10	
74	Backyard Circus	20	
80	Finding Borneo	2	
85	Roller Coaster 1	2	
85	Roller Coaster 2	5	
87	Fun Sponge	5	
97	Curl Shapes	61	
108	Bumper Stickers	2	
113	Read about Bigfoot	5	
116	Bigfoot Stakeout	20	
		180	

Total Possible Points

Your Big
Fat Total

JUN 22 REC'D